The
A–Z
of
Calm

An Hachette UK Company
www.hachette.co.uk

Vie Books, an imprint of Summersdale Publishers
Part of Octopus Publishing Group Limited
Carmelite House
50 Victoria Embankment
LONDON
EC4Y 0DZ
UK

www.summersdale.com

This FSC® label means that materials used for the product have been responsibly sourced

MIX
Paper | Supporting
responsible forestry
FSC® C018236

The authorized representative in the EEA is Hachette Ireland, 8 Castlecourt Centre, Castleknock Road, Castleknock, Dublin 15, D15 YF6A, Ireland.

Printed and bound in Poland

ISBN: 978-1-83799-008-5

Substantial discounts on bulk quantities of Summersdale books are available to corporations, professional associations and other organizations. For details contact general enquiries: telephone: +44 (0) 1243 771107 or email: enquiries@summersdale.com.

The
A–Z
of
Calm

*How to Feel Peaceful
Every Day*

Anna Barnes

vie

Introduction

In a world so full of noise and activity, where busyness seems to be a competitive sport, it is all too easy to lose sight of the gentle, soothing joy of calm.

Calm is space.

It is a gentle sigh and a confidence that things are OK. Calm is a deep breath and a restful night's sleep with a clear mind and an open heart.

Calm offers respite, which in turn affords you the energy to get up and go again to experience the excitement and exhilaration that makes life worth living. Without calm, without that space and that sigh, you can run out of energy, making life more challenging. By pressing the pause button, you can take a moment to reconnect with yourself and the world around you. Across the pages of this book there are tips, tasks, activities and information to support you physically, mentally, emotionally and spiritually. You don't need to read it from cover to cover; dip in and out as you need

and find something that speaks to you in that moment. Use the suggestions to help you cultivate moments of calm in your day-to-day life and create more space for joy alongside it.

You can choose to invite more calm into your life, turn down the chaos and experience the benefit that calm brings to you and those around you.

is for
Acceptance

No one enjoys experiencing unpleasant emotions such as anxiety, fear or sadness, but if you can recognize what you are feeling and sit with it, rather than try to push it away or suppress it, you might find that you can move through it more easily. Sometimes the first step towards accepting these emotions is to create some distance and look at them from a different perspective.

Imagine the emotion you are struggling with as a glass

ball that you can hold in your hands. Take some time to visualize it. Move it around in your palms, examining it from all angles. Consider its size. Feel its weight. Does it have a colour? Is it warm or cool to touch?

Without judgement, identify what the emotion is – it can be more than one. If you can, give it a name. Look at this emotion for what it is, and instead of fighting it, pay attention to it and consider how you could best react to it.

Taking the time to observe, recognize and accept the emotion can create a bit of distance and may afford the opportunity to consider whether the emotion has a message or a purpose. Over time, this practice can help to lessen the intensity of unpleasant emotions and help you to become more in tune with what triggers them, offering you the space to explore what's behind the feelings. When you view emotions with some distance, you gain clarity and understanding, making emotions easier to move through and to let go of over time.

Use the table below to track the variations in your mood across the course of a week. Sometimes even recognizing that our moods can fluctuate from hour to hour helps us to appreciate that even difficult feelings will pass.

	Morning	Afternoon	Evening
Monday			
Tuesday			
Wednesday			
Thursday			
Friday			
Saturday			
Sunday			

When the week is complete, describe in the space below how acknowledging your feelings every day made you feel.

....

....

....

....

....

....

....

....

....

....

In the madness, you have to find calm.

Lupita Nyong'o

Acceptance

breeds calm

is for
Breathwork

Often, when you are anxious, your breathing may become irregular and shallow, or you can breathe too rapidly and end up hyperventilating – even if you're trying to do the opposite. As the human brain can only fully focus on one thing at a time, giving your attention to your breath is a wonderful technique for restoring calm. Focusing on your breathing and taking slow, deep breaths when experiencing anxiety can help move your mind from whatever is causing you to panic, and encourages you to place your attention elsewhere.

Long, slow, deep breaths with a steady inhalation and exhalation can signal to your parasympathetic systems that it is time for your body to relax, helping decrease anxiety and slow a rapid heartrate, leading to a feeling of calm.

Beginning a breathing practice takes a bit of focus, so it is most effective if you can create a calm, quiet space with as few external distractions as possible. Dim lights, minimal noise and a comfortable place to sit or lie will all help. There are numerous breathing practices, many of which are used in yoga and meditation. Deep breathing is most beneficial when practised daily. With regular practice, breathwork can become an unconscious reaction when anxiety arrives.

Try this breathing exercise.

1. Take a slow, deep breath in through your nose.
2. Notice your belly and upper body expanding.
3. Exhale however you feel comfortable, sighing if that feels natural.
4. Do this for several minutes, paying attention to the rise and fall of your belly.
5. Choose a word to focus on and recite it out loud or in your mind as you exhale. Words such as "calm" or "peaceful" might work well.
6. Imagine your inhale gently sweeping over you.
7. Imagine your exhale blowing away your anxieties and negative thoughts.
8. Any time you get distracted, simply notice this and bring your attention back to your breath and your words.

Just breathe.

In, out.

In, out.

is for
Clarity

If you've ever felt so overwhelmed by your "to-do" list that you've been unable to progress with anything, you'll recognize that that feeling is the enemy of calm.

When you feel overwhelmed, it is as though you have so many tasks, so many thoughts in your mind and topics to consider, that they are all competing with each other for brain space, making it impossible to focus on any one thing. The longer you allow this to continue, the bigger that spiral of overwhelm becomes. As soon as you notice this, and have that moment of clarity, there is an opportunity to make a change; take a moment to pause, accept you are feeling overwhelmed and choose to make a plan. Taking back control and gaining some much needed clarity over your thoughts helps to re-establish a sense of calm.

Sometimes, when you are feeling overwhelmed, the best thing to do is grab a pen and a piece of paper and spend 5 minutes writing down everything on your to-do list, even the tiny things. If they are taking up space in your head, they are worth the space on the page. Once you have finished, consider each item on your list in terms of importance and urgency:

- Must – these tasks have to get done soon
- Should – these tasks are less important than the musts but are still necessary
- Could – these tasks are nice to have completed, if possible
- Would like to – these jobs are the cherry on the cake, but if they are left undone, there's no significant fall-out

Create a to-do list and categorize each item in order of priority. This will give you a great idea of where to start.

Must	Could
✔	✔
✔	✔
✔	✔
✔	✔
✔	✔
✔	✔
✔	✔
Should	**Would like to**
✔	✔
✔	✔
✔	✔
✔	✔
✔	✔
✔	✔
✔	✔

There is no such thing

as time management;

there is only self-management.

Rory Vaden

is for
Dogs

Studies show that time spent with animals has a soothing effect, can lower blood pressure and alleviate feelings of stress and anxiety, promoting a sense of calm and well-being. The rhythmical, repetitive action of stroking an animal has a meditative effect, helping to regulate and slow our breathing, while taking them out for a walk boosts our mood by stimulating the release of endorphins, the body's "feel-good chemicals".

Animals can also be a fantastic distraction; while sometimes it is beneficial to sieve through and examine our feelings, sometimes distraction is the perfect route back to calm. If you don't have the space or time for a pet but want to reap some of those benefits, why not volunteer in an animal shelter for a couple of hours a month? If you have any friends or neighbours with a pet, offer to spend some time getting to know the animal and take them out from time to time, or join a community where you can borrow a dog to take for walks or simply spend time with.

Even if you don't have a dog, we can all learn from their behaviour:

- Take regular exercise: Getting out in nature, even for 15 minutes, provides a shot of vitamin D and helps kick-start the body's production of endorphins.
- Rest and recharge: Animals know when to rest and don't feel bad about it! Periods of activity need to be interspersed with periods of rest. Even a 20-minute power nap can make a significant difference to our mood and productivity levels.

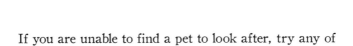

If you are unable to find a pet to look after, try any of these ideas to promote well-being:

- Get out for some exercise and fresh air. Immerse yourself in what you are doing – stop to smell the flowers and really take in your surroundings.
- Engage with others – greet people you meet with warmth.
- Run or play for no other reason than it bringing you joy!
- Enjoy some time doing nothing; have a rest on the sofa without your phone.
- Eat healthy food and drink plenty of water.
- Embrace affection – a hug helps calm the nervous system.
- Sleep.

Animals in our lives

can be a blessing.

J. Wesley Porter

is for
Exercise

Exercise is one of the best medicines to promote good physical and mental health, and it helps you develop resilience and positive self-worth. If we could bottle the side effects of exercise and take it in a tablet, it would be worth a fortune.

Exercise can be anything that requires some physical effort, elevates your heart rate and, if practised over time, can improve the overall health of your body. It's also a great way to release emotional energy.

Walking is great exercise to start with, and it doesn't cost a thing. To begin, try to incorporate short walks into your daily routine: park the car further away or get off the bus a stop earlier. Even a short walk offers the opportunity to clear the mind. Walking has also been proven to improve concentration, improve sleep duration and quality, and reduce the risk of heart disease and stroke. If you lack motivation, try a tracker to log your walks or commit to walking with a friend. You can find great walking groups and routes online.

If walking isn't for you, how about swimming, skipping, dancing or boxing? Check out your local gym, leisure or community centre and see what's available.

Sometimes it is hard to fit exercise into your busy schedule, so why not try to work it around your day-to-day life, such as doing star jumps while you wait for the kettle to boil, or some mild stretching during the ad break of your favourite show?

If you haven't exercised for a while, it might be difficult to figure out what sort of exercise you might enjoy. That lack of clarity can be enough to put you off from trying anything.

Answer the following questions to help narrow down what might suit you.

What sports have I enjoyed in the past?	
What sports do I have an interest in that I would like to try?	
Do I want to exercise alone or with others? Why do I feel this way?	
What motivates me? (e.g. I like competing against myself, I like learning new skills, I would like an opportunity to totally switch off)	

What facilities do I have access to? (e.g. online classes via YouTube or other social media outlets, a local gym or community centre)	
Where can I fit exercise into my day-to-day routine? (e.g. Can I park further away from work? Can I get off the bus a stop or two earlier? Can I go for a walk or swim at lunchtime?)	
What is stopping me from exercising at the moment? This could be emotional and/or physical.	

Get out there
and give it a try;
you might
surprise yourself

Take care of your body.

It's the only place

you have to live.

Jim Rohn

is for
Flow

Flow is the feeling of calm that you get when you're completely engaged in an activity you enjoy or excel at. Time seems to stand still. Athletes sometimes refer to it as being in "the zone".

Typically, humans tend to associate great results with serious effort and, oftentimes, with stress and anxiety. By contrast, flow is that sweet spot where you produce great results with ease.

Lao Tzu, the ancient Chinese philosopher, called it "doing without doing" or "trying without trying".

The activity itself matters far less than the feeling it brings: you aren't clock-watching, you aren't looking for distraction, you are simply absorbed in the task and enjoying it purely for its own sake rather than the result it brings. It is pleasure, not pressure.

An activity that brings this sense of flow will vary from person to person but is often associated with creative tasks or sports; for some it may be something active, like swimming or yoga, for others it may be creative, like singing, colouring or cooking. They key is that it requires focus but feels doable. People who find a state of flow enjoy increased levels of calm, happiness and motivation.

Consider an activity you enjoyed as a child but no longer prioritize. Carve out some time to find the flow and freedom you experienced back then, and feel that sense of pleasure and calm enjoyment return.

To give yourself the greatest chance of finding your flow, first remove all potential distractions. Get yourself a drink and a snack and switch off any unnecessary technology. If possible, put your phone in another room and switch off all nonessential notifications.

Collect any items you need for your task and, if you have a time limit, set an alarm so you can truly switch off until then. Now prepare to lose yourself in a happy state of flow.

May what I do flow

from me like a river, no

forcing and no holding back,

the way it is with children.

Rainer Maria Rilke

is for
Grounding Yourself

When you experience feelings of panic or anxiety it can be all too easy to allow yourself to spiral down towards feeling hopeless and out of control. Next time you notice those pangs of panic rising, fight the urge to add more to that list of possible "what could go wrong" scenarios and instead take a moment to ground yourself.

Grounding is the therapeutic practice of connecting to the energy of the Earth's surface electrons and the natural world around us, absorbing the sights, sounds and smells and engaging all our senses.

Historically, grounding was an everyday occurrence. Lifestyles were simpler and more closely linked with the environment, but advances in technology and home comforts have created a separation between us and the natural world.

Walking barefoot on the ground, feeling the grass beneath your feet, the sand between your toes or the waves lapping at your legs are all grounding practices that help bring you back into the present moment and find calm and strength.

In our busy day-to-day lives it isn't always possible to drive out to the countryside or coast, so finding micromoments for grounding is really important. If you have a garden, spend some time tending some flowers or pulling up weeds. In apartments or urban environments, adding plants to your space helps to bring the outside in and clears the air of pollutants.

Finding a space such as a park or local wildlife centre is another ideal option for connecting with nature and breathing in a sense of calm.

When you recognize feelings of anxiety rising, take a moment to ground yourself back in the present using all of your five senses. First, become aware of your breathing; take some steady deep breaths and take in the environment around you.

Name five things you can see

🌿 .... 🌿 ....
🌿 .... 🌿 ....
🌿 ....

Name four things you can feel

🌿 .... 🌿 ....
🌿 .... 🌿 ....

Name three things you can hear

🌿 .... 🌿 ....
🌿 ....

Name two things you can smell

🌿 ....
🌿 ....

Name one thing you can taste

🌿 ....

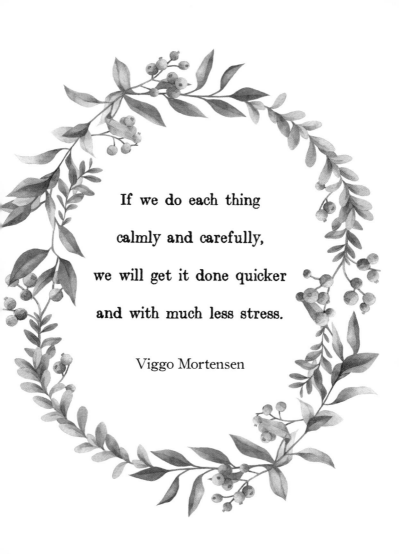

If we do each thing

calmly and carefully,

we will get it done quicker

and with much less stress.

Viggo Mortensen

is for
Hygge

Hygge (pronounced hoo-gah) is the Scandinavian practice of living more simply. It is about inviting calm into your life through minimizing the physical, mental and emotional clutter you may be hanging on to.

In doing so, the things that take up your time each day and that may cause you worry or stress are reduced; there is less to clean, less to care for, less to worry about, and this, in turn, frees you up to pursue habits that bring you peace and joy.

Could you invite a more hygge way of being into your environment? You may not realize it, but your living environment can easily become a stressor. It could be that it is too cluttered; with so many demands on your time, keeping on top of everything can become difficult. By clearing and decluttering, you can reduce stress and create a home where you feel at peace. A calm, positive environment then allows you a safe space to relax after a stressful day.

How can you hygge your habits? Hygge is very much about "less is more", and this extends to activities as well as belongings. Having too many commitments with work, extracurricular activities or even with friends and family can pile on pressure and add stress as opposed to enjoyment. Hygge asks you to reduce these commitments so you can really dedicate yourself and give energy to the ones you choose to keep.

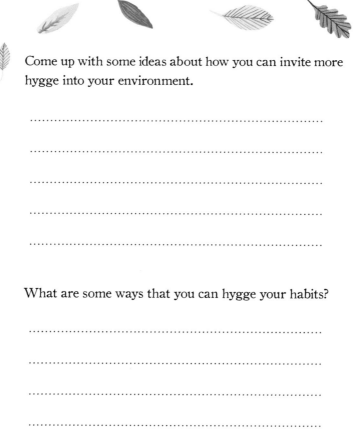

Come up with some ideas about how you can invite more hygge into your environment.

....

....

....

....

....

What are some ways that you can hygge your habits?

....

....

....

....

....

Peace – that was the
other name for home.

Kathleen Norris

is for
Interests

Is there a subject that sparks your interest but that you haven't had the opportunity to explore further? Or a topic you loved at school but left behind when you grew up?

Having an interest or hobby outside of work, home and family is a wonderful way to keep your mind active and provide an alternative focus in times of stress or anxiety. It may also provide an opportunity to develop a new skill, meet new people and make new friends.

Singing, art, reading, gardening and cooking are all known to promote calm and well-being, and all can be enjoyed alone or as part of a group. Cultivating an interest, particularly something creative, allows you to engage the creative network in your brain, which boosts mood and promotes positive self-worth.

Trying anything for the first time (or revisiting something after a period away), particularly as an adult, can be scary but is worth pursuing. Making time to explore your interests is an act of self-care and helps remind you that you are a multifaceted being with many gifts, skills and attributes. If one area of your life is causing you stress or discomfort, there are other areas where you can focus your energy and attention for a while and restore a positive sense of well-being.

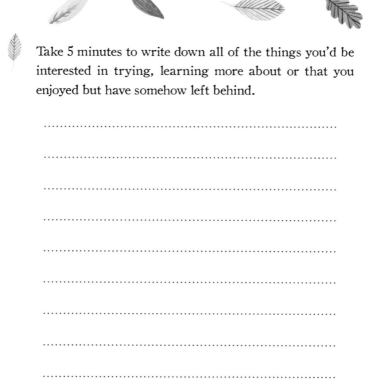

Take 5 minutes to write down all of the things you'd be interested in trying, learning more about or that you enjoyed but have somehow left behind.

....

....

....

....

....

....

....

....

....

Now choose one and commit to trying it in the next month.

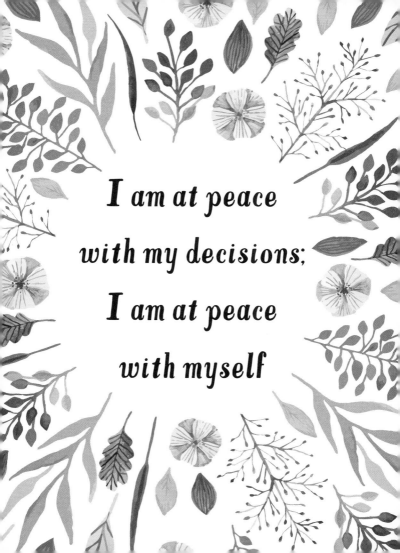

I am at peace
with my decisions;
I am at peace
with myself

is for
Journalling

The average person has more than 6,000 thoughts a day, for example: "What am I going to have for dinner tonight?" or "What time do I need to set the alarm?" These thoughts aren't always constructive; they can be unsupportive and upsetting, for example: "I am not good enough."

If you don't give these thoughts somewhere to be expressed in a constructive way, you can ruminate on them. What should have been a passing question or wondering may become the focus of your time and energy, which can alter your mood and actions and influence how you treat yourself and others.

Having a safe and private space to sieve through these thoughts enables you to look at them more objectively and to reflect on them – what caused me to feel this way? Why did I think that? How would I do things differently next time?

One fantastic outlet for this is journalling. Put simply, this is the writing down of your thoughts and feelings. Regular journalling can help you to become more self-aware and enable you to be more conscious of your choices and decisions. With practice, it affords you the space to choose more positive responses that are more in tune with your values and the person you want to be.

Of course, there are thousands of fancy and expensive journals on the market, but a simple notebook will work just as well. The important thing is putting pen to paper. You can write about your day, your past experiences, your future goals and dreams; nothing is off-limits.

Get yourself a notebook and pen and find a quiet space where you won't be disturbed.

Set your alarm for 5 minutes and commit to writing for the entire time.

Don't think too much or censor yourself – all of your thoughts and feelings are valid.

Use these prompts as a starting point:

- What does happiness mean to me?
- What is something that no one else knows about me?
- My favourite childhood memory is...
- Who plays the biggest role in my life?

Free writing can be challenging to begin with. It might bring up challenging feelings – try to stick with it, but if you find yourself struggling or getting upset, take a break or stop.

Speaking your truth is the most

powerful tool we all have.

Oprah Winfrey

is for
Kindness

Have you ever noticed that when you witness an act of kindness, it produces a fuzzy feel-good sensation in you too?

Kindness is good for you whether you are the recipient or the person doing the good deed, and it even extends to those who witness the act.

One of the greatest benefits of acts of kindness is that they help you recognize the goodness in your own life. Kindness makes you more grateful and promotes empathy and compassion for others. It helps you feel more connected to those around you.

An act of kindness doesn't need to be a grand gesture; it may be as simple as saying hello to someone you pass on the street, giving up your seat on the train or allowing someone to go in front of you at the supermarket or in a traffic jam.

Compassion and kindness are proven to reduce stress, boost your immune system and help reduce negative emotions, including anxiety and depression.

Being kind to others may come more naturally than showing kindness to yourself, but self-compassion is a vital component to paying acts of kindness forward. You cannot pour from an empty cup. When you are feeling stressed, you are less likely to take notice of others around you and to behave in a sensitive and caring way. You create the space for kindness by first treating yourself with kindness and compassion.

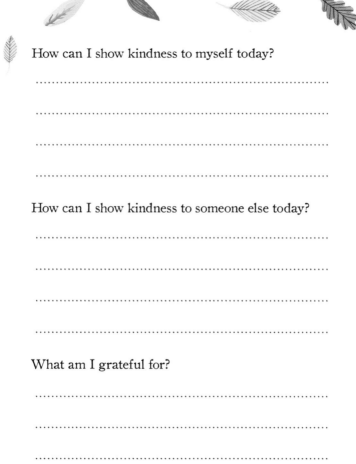

How can I show kindness to myself today?

....

....

....

....

How can I show kindness to someone else today?

....

....

....

....

What am I grateful for?

....

....

....

Kindness is the grease

on the wheels of life

making it a more pleasurable

and worthwhile ride for all

is for
Listening

When your mind is noisy and crowded with thoughts, having somewhere else to direct your focus is really helpful. Listening to a feel-good soundtrack can be a great way to do that.

Listening to music is not only enjoyable; there is also research into the positive effects it can have on your mind and body. While fast, upbeat music can help you to feel more optimistic and energized, a much slower tempo can help to quiet your mind and release tension in your muscles. If you are feeling overwhelmed, playing calming music can be a great way to relax. Some research has shown that it can slow your breathing and heart rate and reduce levels of stress hormones, such as cortisol and adrenaline. There are many calming playlists available on music streaming platforms, but research has shown that the most effective music is that which has been chosen by you. So when you feel the need for some calm, go with what feels good for you and not someone else.

If your anxiety is high but you also have a list of things you have to achieve, a guided podcast might work for you. Gemma Bray is a podcaster who creates guided cleaning sessions to reduce the overwhelm around housework, and she offers a valuable reminder that "good enough" really is good enough. Other bloggers and podcasters offer guided declutter sessions, guided walks, meditations and sessions on working through finances. Whatever the cause of your overwhelm, there is a solution out there for you.

Create your own playlist of music for times when you need to add some calm into your life. When you have chosen your list, why not save it to your phone or computer so you have it to hand when the need arises?

1. ....

2. ....

3. ....

4. ....

5. ....

6. ....

7. ....

8. ....

9. ....

10. ....

Do some research into podcasts that interest you. Write them down in the space below so that the next time you are feeling overwhelmed, they are easily accessible.

1. ....

2. ....

3. ....

4. ....

5. ....

6. ....

7. ....

8. ....

9. ....

10. ....

Music is love and
pain and healing and
joy, all wrapped
up in a melody

Music is the language

of the spirit. It opens the

secret of life bringing peace.

Kahlil Gibran

is for
Mantra

A mantra is a word or phrase repeated multiple times out loud or in your head and is often combined with traditional music. The practice of reciting mantras goes back many thousands of years and originated in India around 1500 BCE. It is widely used in Hinduism, Buddhism and Sikhism and is now becoming more popular the world over as a beautiful and powerful tool to help quiet the mind and generate a more positive mental and emotional state.

The word "mantra" is from Sanskrit and translates as "mind tool". They are considered to be "tools of thought", used as a means of harnessing and focusing the mind. With practice, a mantra can become a powerful and restorative tool that allows the mind to rest and refocus on more compassionate self-talk. It also helps you to stay focused on a positive state of mind, or on emotions like love and forgiveness. In modern usage, the word "mantra" can be compared to a positive affirmation helping to cultivate a sense of calm.

While mantras help calm the mind, they also have a positive effect on the body, as the soothing combination of sound, breath and rhythm has a measurable impact on the parasympathetic nervous system, otherwise known as the "rest and digest" system. This, in turn, slows the heart rate and triggers the body's healing response.

While it is thought that vocalizing the mantra gives it more substance, you can also write them down. Choose your mantra based on what is important to you, for example: "I am a good person", or "I am in control of my own destiny."

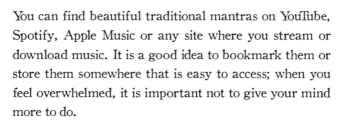

You can find beautiful traditional mantras on YouTube, Spotify, Apple Music or any site where you stream or download music. It is a good idea to bookmark them or store them somewhere that is easy to access; when you feel overwhelmed, it is important not to give your mind more to do.

Write down any mantras that particularly resonate with you, or create your own:

....

....

....

....

....

....

....

....

Chanting is a way of getting

in touch with yourself.

It's an opening of the heart and

letting go of the mind and thoughts.

Krishna Das

is for
Night Sky

Gazing up at a dark sky covered in a blanket of stars can be an incredibly calming activity. The dark, the quiet, the incredible space between you and the rest of the universe. It is magnificent. You are not limited to just seeing stars – at certain times during the year, planets will be easier to see with the naked eye, and there may be meteor showers, eclipses or shooting stars. You can find out more about what you can see wherever you are in the world using an app to identify the stars and planets, or with a simple internet search. Still, as with all things, you are at the mercy of the elements, so rain or clouds could hamper your view.

The simple act of looking up to the sky can be a great way to reconnect with nature and find your inner calm. Sometimes it is so easy to get bogged down with the humdrum of everyday life that you forget that you are part of something far greater than the Earth we inhabit. Slow down and take a break from the constant demands of life, and find a moment to be more present. While looking to the sky, feel the tension in your mind and body start to loosen as you put your worries into perspective.

Are there any constellations in particular you'd like to see? Why not do some research and see if you can find them in the night sky?

If there is significant light pollution where you are, consider a visit to a dark park or planetarium to see the skies more clearly.

....

....

....

....

....

....

....

....

Use this space to sketch or jot down any constellations you spot in the night sky.

We are all

made of stars

Keep your eyes

on the stars but

remember to keep your

feet on the ground.

Theodore Roosevelt

is for
Organization

One of the best ways to encourage a sense of calm in your everyday life is to develop the tools and confidence you'll need to handle whatever curve balls life throws your way.

One of the most valuable of those tools is taking the time to become more organized. It isn't cool or sexy, but it will absolutely make a positive difference.

Have you ever left things to the very last minute – and

felt an ever-tightening knot in your stomach because you have something coming up that you aren't ready for? Whether that is handing in a report, a meal with the in-laws or a birthday party you forgot to organize, the sensation is the same and it is anything but calm.

Pre-planning and organization afford you space – both mental and physical. They allow you the head space to be flexible. Having an idea of how you want an event or activity to go means that you aren't thrown off course with every new idea or suggestion. It provides a direction of travel without it needing to be a military operation timed to the second.

Planning doesn't need to squeeze out the fun and spontaneity of life. Ironically, taking the time to get organized gives you back the head space to enjoy the event because the thinking has been done in advance. Phew!

Consider an event or activity you have coming up. What can you organize in advance to take the pressure off the day and allow you to enjoy the event?

Event/Activity:

....

Plan of Action:

....

....

....

....

....

....

....

....

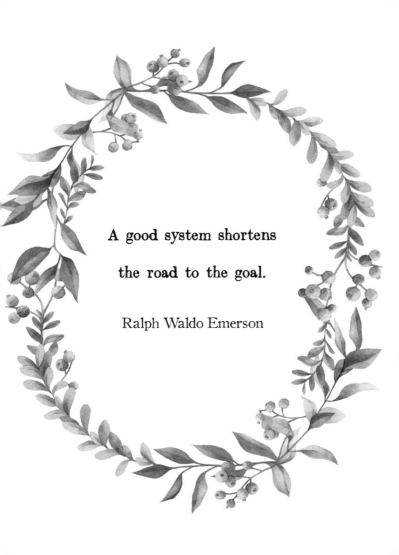

A good system shortens

the road to the goal.

Ralph Waldo Emerson

is for
Puzzles

Puzzles, whether they are word puzzles, number puzzles or jigsaw puzzles, are a wonderful way to give your brain a task to help refocus you and reduce feelings of anxiety.

Sitting with a cup of tea and a puzzle is the perfect activity to stretch your brain, quiet your mind and provide a positive focus to prevent rumination and catastrophizing.

You can find hundreds of brain training puzzles online, but why not use this as an excuse to step away from technology and pick up a traditional puzzle book, or to find the puzzle pages in a newspaper? That way you are less likely to be distracted by updates and notifications and can really immerse yourself in the task at hand. In addition to focusing your mind and reducing your stress levels, spending 10 minutes each day working on puzzles can help to maintain brain function and may reduce the risk of diseases such as dementia.

While puzzling can be a meditative activity done in solitude, it can also be a great way to reconnect with family and friends. If you are looking to expand your social circle, you could also see if there are any games centres in your community. The shared feeling of accomplishment is a fantastic bonding exercise!

Why not make yourself a drink and take a 10-minute break to complete this word search? All of the words should remind you of the value of calm.

CALM	KINDNESS	SELF-CARE
GRATITUDE	PEACE	SLEEP
INTERESTS	PUZZLES	WELLNESS
JOY	REST	YOGA

D	A	J	D	X	B	W	S	E	L	F	C	A	R	E
A	Q	J	Q	A	J	E	I	W	O	M	K	T	Q	R
M	R	F	T	I	O	L	N	D	D	U	D	B	S	W
O	X	E	T	P	Y	L	F	M	Q	C	A	L	M	K
Y	K	W	F	B	J	N	O	N	T	U	D	I	E	I
N	W	A	V	U	R	E	S	L	E	E	P	B	Z	N
C	H	T	L	Y	M	S	M	R	M	P	M	N	V	D
P	U	Z	Z	L	E	S	J	D	G	W	H	V	R	N
O	E	H	S	E	Q	K	A	O	D	R	J	M	E	E
D	J	F	C	I	N	T	E	R	E	S	T	S	S	S
F	E	Q	E	W	U	N	N	D	V	D	E	Y	T	S
O	W	X	N	P	E	A	C	E	J	J	O	O	R	K
G	R	A	T	I	T	U	D	E	W	L	U	G	Z	B
R	C	K	L	G	Z	Y	X	X	J	L	M	A	H	R
F	K	Q	K	F	X	M	Y	R	F	D	W	Y	X	S

What you surround yourself with should bring you peace of mind and peace of spirit.

Stacy London

is for
Question Your Thoughts

You have thoughts about yourself: some of them are positive, and some of them are negative. The latter can be harmful and threaten your sense of calm, for example: "I could never do that", "I'm too shy, too anxious...", or (insert your own limiting belief here). These are called ANTs (Automatic Negative Thoughts).

It's really important to consider these ANTs critically. Questioning their validity can help break these, often habitual, ways of thinking, as they can often cause a lot of stress and hold you back in life. It's also important to remember that, just because you think these things, that doesn't make them true. Next time you experience a negative thought about yourself, consider the following:

- What are you doing and who are you with when you have this thought?
- Consider what evidence you have to prove this thought is actually true.
- Consider what evidence you have to challenge or disprove this thought.
- On a scale of 1 to 10, what is the genuine likelihood of this happening?
- What is the worst thing that could happen?
- How could you cope with that?
- How is this way of thinking impacting your life?
- What would be a more accurate or objective way of thinking?

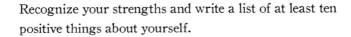

Recognize your strengths and write a list of at least ten positive things about yourself.

1. ....

2. ....

3. ....

4. ....

5. ....

6. ....

7. ....

8. ....

9. ....

10. ....

Peace can't be achieved

in the outside world unless

we have peace on the inside.

Goldie Hawn

is for
Real Rest

Rest is more than simply sitting on the sofa, vegging out in front of the TV while simultaneously scrolling on your phone. Real rest feeds and revives you physically, mentally and emotionally.

It is deep enough that your nervous system allows your stress response to switch off, helping your whole being to reset. Now, when was the last time you did that?

When we are rested, we are more positive, resilient,

effective and calm. When we are drained, we can be the opposite; irritable and anxious – we struggle to think rationally and make good decisions and we are more likely to snap at others, so the impact can be far reaching. Not everyone can take a week off for a holiday or have a weekend spa break every time they're feeling overwhelmed, so enjoying small, sustainable micro-rests throughout the day and week are the best way to keep on top of things, even if it's taking just 5 minutes to practise a breathing technique. There are different types of rest that can help to bring back calm and balance. The type of rest you need depends on the kind of day you've had, or if you haven't rested for a while, you might be depleted in all areas.

There are up to ten types of rest that are recognized; the one you need most depends on the kind of stress you've experienced over the course of the day or week. Here are the four most common types of rest:

- Physical: When your body feels physically tired and you need to take time to help your body recover. For this, yoga or a nap can be a good way of taking rest.
- Mental: When your brain feels overloaded with obligations, work tasks, life admin and to-dos. For this, taking time for a "flow" activity could be beneficial.
- Emotional: When you are carrying overwhelming emotions that you struggle to impart. Talk therapy or a get-together with friends where you can discuss your feelings is a great way to overcome these problems.
- Social: If you have a lot of caring commitments and are giving a lot to others, social rest is the opportunity to spend time with others who uplift you and refill your cup. Spend time with those who make you feel better simply by being in their presence. This is a place where you feel seen, accepted and you are free to be completely yourself.

Which of these types of rest feels most relevant for you at the moment?

....

What can you do to recharge yourself in each of these areas, and what steps do you need to take to carve out the time for this?

....

....

....

....

....

....

....

....

....

Rest awhile —

the world can wait.

You see it best when

you view it refreshed.

To prevent fatigue and worry,

the first rule is rest often.

Rest before you get tired.

Dale Carnegie

is for
Stirring

Repetitive motion can be a great way to redirect your focus away from anxiety and stress. When engaging in a repetitive action, such as stirring food, your mind can eventually slip away from any worries you have in that moment, into a calmer, more passive state. The benefits provided by repeated actions to calm the mind mean that preparing foods that require a lot of stirring, such as a risotto or porridge, can provide just the right balance of focus and repetition to quiet an anxious mind (and there is the tasty added benefit of the soporific carbohydrate hit at the end!).

Cooking not only has the benefit of the repetitive actions of stirring, it is also a fantastic stress reliever in itself. Food preparation can often be overlooked, with the quickest and easiest option often chosen over the slower, more rewarding path.

Cooking allows you the chance to slow down and create something enjoyable, engaging all your senses in the process. From the physical act of chopping and stirring, to how the meal tastes, the textures, the aroma, the sounds and the visual effects that you can create – these are all things that can easily be taken for granted when making a meal.

Cooking can also be a great way to reconnect with friends or family, to discuss your day as you prepare the food, and to come together to eat.

Next time you make a meal, take notice of your five senses and write down what you experience.

See:

....

Smell:

....

Taste:

....

Touch:

....

Hear:

....

How did the act of mindfully cooking and eating make you feel?

....

The ritual of
cooking feeds
the soul as much
as the body

is for
Toolbox

When your mind is clouded and your thoughts are jumbled, it can be really difficult to find a way out of the mire. A toolbox – a physical box containing items to help lift your mood and clear the fog – is a wonderful article, as it allows us to give our brain a break; we do not need to think of something to soothe us when the darkness descends, as the solutions are in the box. The contents of this box will be personal to you, and the box is best created when you're feeling good, as you don't want to be doing this when you are feeling anxious – our minds have enough to contend with when anxiety strikes. The aim of the toolbox is to jump-start your brain to move away from the negative thoughts.

The box doesn't need to be anything expensive or fancy – a plain shoebox will do. Spend time decorating your box with photographs, positive quotes, images of places or items that are personal to you. Inside your box, add items that will calm you. Popular ideas are a calming scent, such as lavender, a music playlist, photos of loved ones or colouring books to refocus your mind on something else. You may also like to add items like a fidget spinner, stress ball or other fidget-specific tools that are designed to relieve anxiety and calm the mind.

Don't feel like you have to get it all done at once; you can fill the box over time and swap things in and out as your preferences change.

This box is your route back to calm. Call on it whenever you need, and be gentle with yourself in these challenging moments. They will pass.

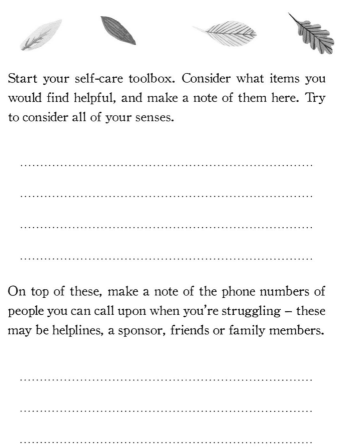

Start your self-care toolbox. Consider what items you would find helpful, and make a note of them here. Try to consider all of your senses.

....

....

....

....

On top of these, make a note of the phone numbers of people you can call upon when you're struggling – these may be helplines, a sponsor, friends or family members.

....

....

....

....

You cannot perceive beauty

but with a serene mind.

Henry David Thoreau

is for
Understanding

We share a planet with 8 billion other human beings. Day to day, we interact with other people; they may be friends, family, colleagues or strangers.

Like you, each of these people will have their own experiences, their own triggers and traumas and their own baggage, which sometimes can cause them to treat you unfairly or to be unkind. This behaviour is very rarely about us. What a relief. Understanding this is really liberating and can help offer some distance between the interactions you have with others and how it lands with you.

The next time someone speaks to you or behaves in a way that upsets or unsettles you, take a minute to recognize that it is not about you. Remind yourself that you don't have to take that negative energy in. You can decide to recognize that their behaviour is a result of their own experiences and not yours.

Instead of becoming riled up by their behaviour and allowing it to impact negatively on your day, try to empathize with them. Life is complex and multilayered. Treating people with kindness and empathy and allowing breathing space to consider your response is like a pebble in a pond. The ripples of a conscious, considered and kind response help make the world a more positive place. None of us are alone in our struggles.

The next time you are upset by someone else's behaviour, try this forgiveness meditation:

1. Sit somewhere quiet where you won't be disturbed, close your eyes and focus on your breathing.
2. Bring a picture of the person who upset you into your mind.
3. As you picture them, repeat the mantra, "I do not hold on to resentment, I forgive and move on."
4. If painful or angry thoughts come up, try to notice them and return to the mantra.
5. Imagine the anger leaving your body with each exhalation.
6. Try to continue this for 5 minutes or until the feelings subside.

Be kind, for everyone

you meet is fighting a battle

you know nothing about.

Wendy Mass

is for
Vision Boarding

Sometimes not knowing what you want out of life can feel daunting and provoke anxiety. Life can get busy and you can lose track of what you are aiming for, so having somewhere to visually represent what you want for the future can be an excellent way to calm and focus the mind. Spending time creating your own vision board is a beautiful act of self-care; it is an opportunity to reflect on what brings you joy and peace, what you want more or less of in your life, and it allows you to visualize and dream about the future you wish to create for yourself. You can add anything you want to your vision board – a postcard representing your dream holiday destination, magazine cuttings that speak of what you want for the future or simply inspirational quotes to help motivate you. The possibilities are endless!

The power in the board comes from the clarity the images provide. Spending time considering deeply what you want from your future – be that the next six weeks, a year or five years down the road – is a powerful practice, and revisiting those words and images on a daily basis means that they become deeply ingrained in your day-to-day choices and actions.

Before you sit down to create your physical vision board, you need to get clear on what your goals are and why they matter to you. People sometimes divide their goals up into categories of health and well-being, relationships, work, finance, travel and home – it is completely up to you – it's your future!

Make your own vision board.

You will need:
- A large cork board or piece of card
- Pictures, postcards, inspiring quotes, cuttings from magazines – anything that can be stuck down that represents your dreams!
- Scissors
- Glue or sticky tape
- Pens and/or pencils
- Imagination!

1. Get a clear idea of your goals and find visual representations of them to stick onto your board.
2. Before sticking them down, organize them on your board in a way that is clear and easy for you to see – try not to clutter it up too much.
3. Hang your board somewhere private but prominent for you.
4. Spend some time actively looking at your board each day.

Your vision is your
truth and your power.
Show it clearly, even
if only to yourself.

is for
White Noise

We live in a noisy world! There is always something going on, whatever time of the day or night. Activity creates noise, and excessive or unwanted noise, especially at bedtime, can cause a huge amount of stress and anxiety. There are practical ways to block out many night-time sounds, such as closing the windows, putting in ear plugs or investing in noise-cancelling headphones. One other solution is white noise. White noise has been clinically proven to reduce anxiety by weakening the link between sound and a stress response. It covers our complete sound spectrum, which means it is a really excellent mask for other noises. Simply put, it acts as a sort of shock absorber, blocking other sounds that your brain may otherwise be unable to ignore. White noise falls into two categories: natural (such as a waterfall or raindrops) and artificial (sounds like the whir of a washing machine or the continuous hum of a vacuum cleaner).

While excessive noise can be stress-provoking, so can silence. While it can be incredibly relaxing in some situations, the sound of silence can also act as a microphone for your thoughts, as there is nothing to distract your mind or switch your focus. White noise, or a sound from somewhere else on the spectrum – pink, brown or grey – can give your brain somewhere else to go, allowing your thoughts to quiet and a sense of calm to lull you to sleep.

Use this table to note down your findings and rate how calm the sounds made you feel, with one being really calm and ten being not calm at all.

Sound	Where it was found (natural, website, app)	Calm rating (1–10)

For fast-acting relief,

try slowing down.

Lily Tomlin

is for
Xanthite

Crystals and gemstones are precious or semi-precious stones made of minerals, organic matter or fossils formed over millions of years and shaped by volcanic heat and waters. Xanthite is just one example and is a manganese-rich gemstone believed to help ward off fear and melancholy.

Crystal healing has a long and rich history, with these precious stones being used for a number of healing practices by cultures all over the world. Today, using crystals and gemstones to promote and enhance particular emotions is a popular movement, and there is a crystal or gemstone to help with whatever challenges or worries you face. Popular crystals that promote calm and help alleviate anxiety include:

- Amethyst
- Celestite
- Rose quartz
- Howlite
- Black tourmaline

Learning about crystals and gemstones is an interesting and accessible hobby that fits perfectly with the practices of mindfulness, meditation and cultivating a calmer life.

You can buy gems online or search for crystal stores local to you. Select a couple that you feel drawn to and then take some time to familiarize yourself with them – their weight in your hand, their smoothness or edges, their colourings at different times of the day.

Try this crystal mindfulness practice the next time life feels overwhelming.

1. Sit down with your bare feet flat on the floor (you may wish to lean against a wall for comfort).
2. Place a crystal of your choosing underneath each foot.
3. Take time to get used to the feel of the crystal on the soles of your feet.
4. Close your eyes or soften your gaze and breathe slowly and deeply: in through your nose and out through your mouth.
5. Imagine the light and energy of the crystals penetrating your feet and travelling up all the way through your body until you are filled with light and energy.

Be the energy you want others to absorb.

A. D. Posey

is for
Yoga

The ancient practice of yoga is about far more than the postures and poses – it is a way of being, a mindset.

The Western world often uses yoga as a form of physical fitness – but to practise at this level is to miss the essence of yoga altogether.

Yoga is as much about what happens off the mat as on it, perhaps more so. The yoga mindset is about acceptance of yourself, your situation and others. In essence, becoming a yogi (someone who practises yoga consistently) is about embodying humility, practising mindfulness, empathy and kindness, throughout all aspects of life. It is a simple concept but not an easy one to master.

If you are a relatively fit and flexible person, a standard yoga class where each pose is completed individually – often referred to as hatha yoga – is a good place to start. Once you have settled into a regular practice, you can explore other disciplines, such as vinyasa, or "flow yoga", where the poses are all completed in a sequence. The key is to start slowly; don't worry about what the other students are doing or what you managed last time. Each class is a new experience and learning opportunity. What your body was comfortable with last time may not be the same next time, so take it easy and treat yourself with compassion.

One of the simplest yoga poses you can learn is Savasana, typically used at the end of a class leading into a meditation. Try it when you need a moment of calm.

1. Find a safe, warm and comfortable place to lie down on your back.
2. Let your arms and legs gently drop open. Your arms should be at a 45-degree angle from your body, but do whatever feels comfortable for you.
3. If there is any strain on your lower back, place a bolster or folded blanket under your knees.
4. Close your eyes and pay attention to your breathing, while letting your body completely relax.
5. Consciously take note of how your body feels while letting it move into a state of total relaxation.
6. Stay in this position for 5 to 15 minutes.
7. When you feel you are finished, start to wiggle your fingers and toes to slowly awaken your body before sitting up.

N.B. If you are pregnant, consult with your doctor before trying any yoga poses.

Yoga is not about

self-improvement,

it's about self-acceptance.

Gurmukh Kaur Khalsa

is for
Zzzzzz

Anxiety is exhausting, and when you are tired, thinking logically and having the capacity to make good choices to help embrace calm is all the harder. It is easy to fall into a downward spiral leading to low mood and increasing levels of anxiety. It's a catch-22.

So, what's the secret to settling down to a restful, resetting night's sleep? Routine! Setting yourself a regular "route to bedtime" has been proven to make a significant difference to drifting off to sleep. Try adding a couple of the following ideas to your evening routine:

- Dim the lights – avoiding screens and blue light for at least 30 minutes before bed prompts the body to begin producing melatonin, a hormone to encourage sleep. It also means you are less likely to doom scroll on social media, giving your brain a break before bed.
- Take a bath – a warm bath before bed can relax muscles and joints and help reduce stress and anxiety in the body.
- Enjoy a light read (with a real book) – using a hard copy of a book as opposed to reading on a tablet means you can avoid screens and technology before bed.
- Write it down – keep a notebook and pen by your bed and use them to jot down any worries or tasks that are playing on your mind.
- Background babble – if your thoughts persist, try a guided meditation or white noise to help you place your focus outside of your own chatter.

Try an activity to relax your brain and body.

1. Making sure your room is dimly lit, lie down in bed and make yourself comfortable.
2. Close your eyes and scrunch up your toes for the count of three before releasing them. Moving systematically around your body, complete the scrunch and release for all of your muscles. Make sure each part feels really relaxed and heavy before you move on.
3. You may start to feel heavy, tingly and almost numb. This is your body preparing for sleep.
4. Focus on breathing slowly, deeply and comfortably, repeating to yourself "in, out, in, out" in your mind until you slowly fall asleep.

There is a time for many words,

and there is also a time for sleep.

Homer

Conclusion

Cultivating calm takes practice; it is a state of mind that needs nurturing. It is possible to live a calm life even when things feel busy and chaotic – it is your response to what is happening that creates the calm or amplifies the anxiety.

No one gets it right all the time; it is the coming back and the trying again that will develop your skills and strengthen your mind for a calmer outlook.

Throughout the pages of this book there are lessons and nuggets of wisdom to hopefully open up more opportunities for your own learning, self-discovery and acceptance.

It is this leaning in, learning, growing and understanding of ourselves, our past, our plans, dreams and desires that afford us the space and clarity for calm.

Self-care is not something that should be saved for emergencies, when you are feeling emotionally depleted and anxious. It takes discipline, and it means choosing yourself so your emotional cup doesn't empty. Treat yourself as you would a friend: with patience, empathy and love.

In understanding ourselves more fully, we quiet the external noise that can knock us off course.

Breathe in and enjoy an abundant life of calm in the chaos.

Do not mistake
calm for dull.
The space that
calm creates allows
magic to happen.

Within you, there is a stillness

and a sanctuary to which you can

retreat at any time and be yourself.

Hermann Hesse

The A–Z of Mindfulness

Anna Barnes

ISBN: 978-1-78783-273-2

Hardback

Squeeze every drop out of each moment and live life to the full by discovering the art of mindfulness. Learn new ways to connect with yourself and the world around you and reignite a sense of wonder in the everyday with this practical ABC of illustrated tips for mindful living.

The A–Z of Positivity

Anna Barnes

ISBN: 978-1-80007-704-1

Hardback

There's magic in making the best out of a bad situation, no matter
what life throws at you. Luckily, there are plenty of little things you
can do to brighten your outlook and bring a ray of sunshine to every
moment. This charming A–Z guide will help your inner optimist
thrive, and show you how to bring more positivity into every day.

The A–Z of Wellbeing

Anna Barnes

ISBN: 978-1-80007-705-8

Hardback

The things that add up to a happier life don't have to
be complicated. Whether you choose to dance and sing,
give yoga a go or tap into the power of quietude and
kindness, this charming A–Z guide will help you find
your perfect path towards a greater sense of wellbeing.

Image Credits

pp. 3, 11, 33, 45, 68, 69, 99, 103, 128
© Anastasia Panfilova/Shutterstock.com

Spots on chapter pages throughout
© Alena Tselesh/Shutterstock.com

Letter heads throughout
© Maslova Larisa/Shutterstock.com

Background pp. 41, 113 © Anassia Art/Shutterstock.com

Background pp. 10, 77 © Rolau Elena/Shutterstock.com

pp. 5, 53, 86, 109 © VerisStudio/Shutterstock.com

pp. 28, 58, 91, 124 © VerisStudio/Shutterstock.com

pp. 23, 59, 87, 121 © Nikiparonak/Shutterstock.com

pp. 29, 63, 95, 125 © Nikiparonak/Shutterstock.com

pp. 19, 49, 81, 117 © Tatiana Goncharuk/Shutterstock.com

If you're interested in finding
out more about our books, find us
on Facebook at *Summersdale Publishers,*
on Twitter/X at *@Summersdale* and on
Instagram and TikTok at *@Summersdalebooks*
and get in touch. We'd love to hear from you.

www.summersdale.com